Facts About the Piranha

By Lisa Strattin

© 2019 Lisa Strattin

Facts for Kids Picture Books by Lisa Strattin

Little Blue Penguin, Vol 92

Chipmunk, Vol 5

Frilled Lizard, Vol 39

Blue and Gold Macaw, Vol 13

Poison Dart Frogs, Vol 50

Blue Tarantula, Vol 115

African Elephants, Vol 8

Amur Leopard, Vol 89

Sabre Tooth Tiger, Vol 167

Baboon, Vol 174

Sign Up for New Release Emails Here

http://LisaStrattin.com/subscribe-here

Monthly Surprise Box

http://KidCraftsByLisa.com

Contents

INTRODUCTION

The piranha is a type of freshwater fish found in the rivers of the South American jungles. They can be found in nearly every country in South America and have been appearing more recently in the southern states of the USA.

CHARACTERISTICS

The piranha has one single row of razor-sharp teeth and are most commonly known for their desire and hunt for blood. They feed on fish, mammals and birds, with the whole group of piranhas feeding together in what is called a "feeding frenzy."

APPEARANCE

The piranha is a relatively small fish with a round body, large head, and bulldog-like face.

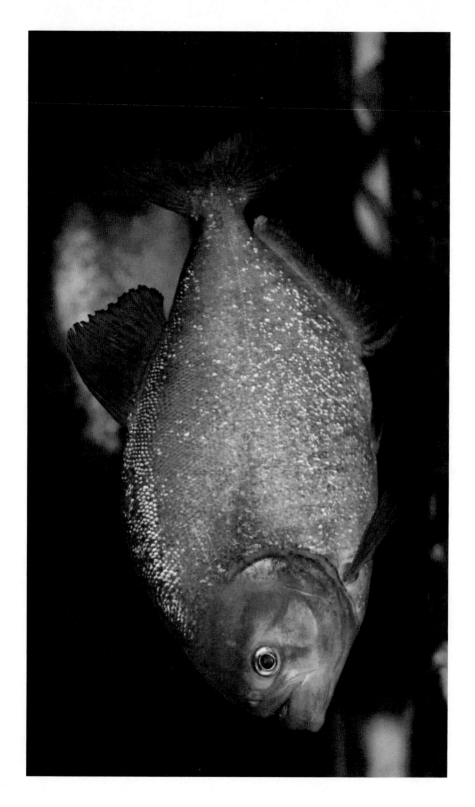

12

BREEDING

Piranhas tend to breed in pairs in slow-moving water like lagoons, during the rainy season where they live, around April to May. The mating pair prepare a nest where the female lays her clusters of eggs. She lays an average of 5,000 eggs and because the male and female both defend their eggs so fiercely, more than 90% of them often survive and hatch after just a few days.

LIFE SPAN

Piranha have been known to live between 20 to 25 years!

SIZE

The piranha is generally around 8 to 20 inches long. Supposedly people are more afraid of piranhas than many other marine animals, even sharks!

HABITAT

Piranhas are found in fast flowing rivers and streams where there is plenty of food for the piranha to eat, except during mating season. The piranhas live together in large shoals and constantly compete with each other for food. Feeding frenzies will be triggered when there is a shortage of food for them or when they find blood in the water.

DIET

Despite the carnivorous nature of the piranha, they are actually omnivores and will eat almost anything they can find. They mainly feed on fish, snails, insects and aquatic plants, while occasionally eating larger mammals and birds that fall into the water.

ENEMIES

Despite their feared nature, the piranha actually have a number of predators in the wild, including humans that hunt the piranha for food. They are preyed upon by large predators like the river dolphins, crocodiles, turtles, birds and larger fish.

SUITABILITY AS PETS

Piranhas can make interesting pets with their sharp teeth and their fast and furious attack skills. Their food and environment needs (water temperature, etc.) are simple to maintain.

Keeping piranhas is a bigger commitment than keeping other kinds of fish as pets, though. They require lots of space, and they can live more than 20 years in captivity. So, if you want to keep a piranha, you should talk to other folks who can give you the guidance you need to prepare the appropriate tank for them.

COLOR ME

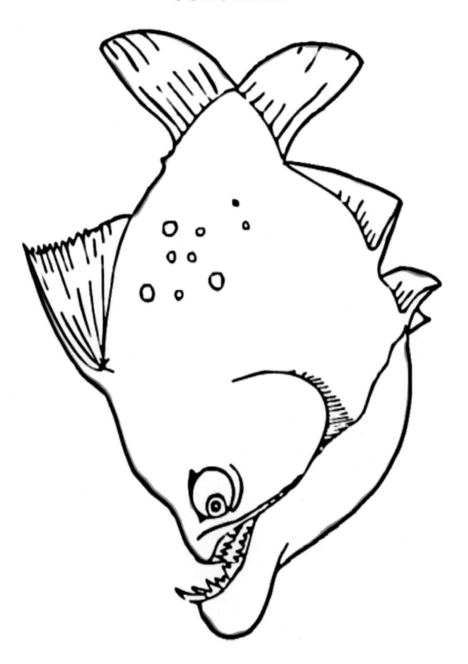

COLOR ME

COLOR ME

COLOR ME

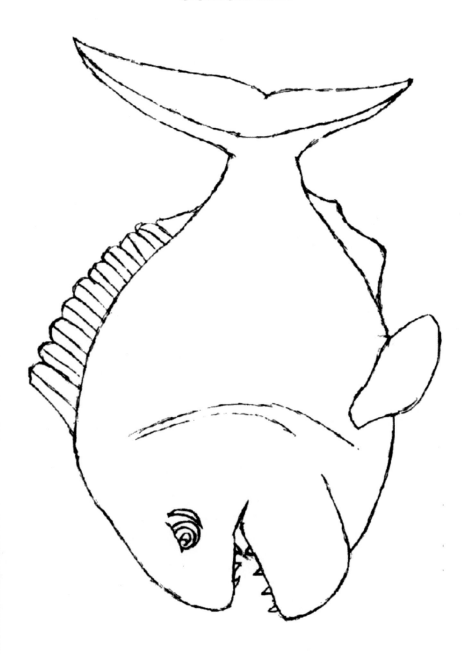

COLOR ME

COLOR ME

COLOR ME

COLOR ME

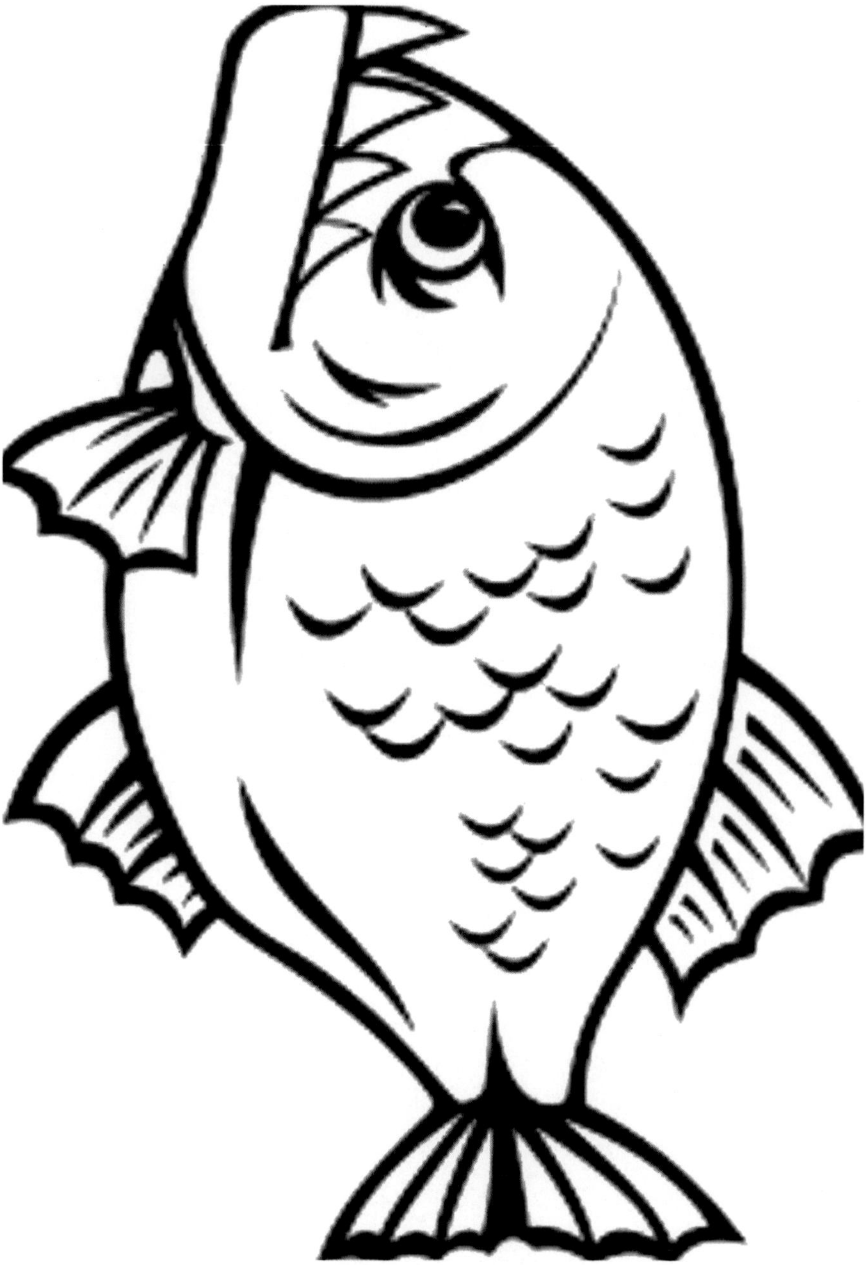

Please leave me a review here:

http://lisastrattin.com/Review-Vol-264

For more Kindle Downloads Visit Lisa Strattin Author Page on Amazon Author Central

http://amazon.com/author/lisastrattin

To see upcoming titles, visit my website at LisaStrattin.com– all books available on kindle!

http://lisastrattin.com

PLUSH PIRANHA TOY

You can get one by copying and pasting this link into your browser:

http://lisastrattin.com/PlushPiranha

MONTHLY SURPRISE BOX

Get yours by copying and pasting this link into your browser

http://KidCraftsByLisa.com

Made in the USA
Middletown, DE
10 January 2020

82987927R00022